DOWN TO THE SEA

WITH

JACK WOODSON

The Artistry of a Distinguished
American Illustrator

Text by

WILLIAM L. TAZEWELL

With a Preface by

VIRGINIUS DABNEY

Algonquin Books of Chapel Hill

1987

DOWN TO THE SEA

WITH

JACK WOODSON

Published by
Algonquin Books of Chapel Hill
Post Office Box 2225
Chapel Hill, North Carolina 27515-2225

in association with
Taylor Publishing Company
1550 West Mockingbird Lane
Dallas, Texas 75235

For permission to reproduce certain illustrations by Jack Woodson in this book, the artist and the publisher are grateful to the United States Historical Society, Bleecker Street Publishing Corporation, United States Navy, Carmine Foods, Life Insurance Company of Virginia, Mariners' Museum, Baptist Foreign Mission Board, Royal Copenhagen/Bing and Grondahl, Flying Cloud Restaurant, Standard Paper Manufacturing Company.

Library of Congress Cataloging-in-Publication Data
Tazewell, William L., 1932–
    Down to the sea with Jack Woodson.

    1. Woodson, Jack.   2. Sea in art.   3. Ships in art.   4. Marine painting, American.   5. Marine painting—20th century—United States.   I. Woodson, Jack.   II. Title.
ND237.W815A4   1987   759.13   87-1296
ISBN 0-912697-63-6

LIST OF ILLUSTRATIONS

Color Illustrations

Black and White Illustrations

PREFACE

BY VIRGINIUS DABNEY

The foundation for John Waddie Woodson's career as an authentic portrayer of the majesty and mystery of the sea and the ships that sail upon it was laid in his youth. Although born in Richmond, he spent his summers for years in the Norfolk area. He built boats with his own hands and sailed them often out of sight of land.

Many artists and writers have sought over the centuries to portray the sea in its many moods. The Psalmist wrote of those "that go down to the sea in ships, that do business in great waters," while Homer hymned "the wine-dark sea," and Eugene O'Neill "dat ole devil sea."

Jack Woodson's household gods are two Dutchmen—JanVermeer, whose paintings are so marvelously true to life, and Willem Van de Velde, Holland's masterful marine artist. These men exhibit the same capacity for detail, accompanied by a genius for total accuracy, that Woodson displays in his canvases.

Woodson has painted and preserved eras of the sea—the sailing ships, the workboats, the harbor tugs, the fishing skipjacks and bugeyes, the cargo ships, the river packets that used to patrol Virginia rivers before the railroads made them obsolete. His canvases are enormously detailed and authentic, completely documentary; yet they are more than photography; they seem to glow with the luminosity of what the Germans call *Dinglichkeit*, absolute fidelity to the subject.

From the time when, at age ten, Woodson began art classes, and then in the Great Depression had the opportunity to turn out artwork in the basement of the old Loew's Theater in Richmond, he has been truly dedicated. William L. Tazewell points out in the accompanying text that as a youngster at Loew's he was so passionately devoted to his task that he often worked until 2 or 3 A.M., and even then didn't want to quit. He has shown much the same devotion ever since. Today, at age 74, he seldom takes vacations.

Furthermore, he has achieved his goals. His work is sought in many parts of this country and abroad. He paints for institutions and individuals and gives them what they want. The present volume affords many examples of his virtuosity as a painter of ships and the sea, but his subjects also include artwork for television and motion pictures, murals for buildings, illustrations for books, Christmas cards for organizations, and depictions of historical events. These last are particularly notable for their scholarly qualities, since with these canvases, based on vast research, he has recreated history. The Battle of the Capes, Washington firing the first shot at the siege of Yorktown, events of the Civil War and the two World Wars are all brought to life in his paintings. So is the American West, with its outlaws and sheriffs and lawmen. He has an eye for detail, the sharp line, and the sweep of motion, as well as the accommodating curvature and uniqueness of separate objects. It is no exaggeration to say that, in a kind of retrospective, Jack Woodson has recreated nearly sixty years of American and Virginia life.

Ultra-sophisticated critics are wont to deprecate such artists as "mere illustrators." The fact that many of these same critics regard Andy Warhol with his Campbell Soup cans as a giant of the art world provides considerable balm for Jack Woodson's soul.

Woodson has chosen to live and work in his native Richmond rather than accept tempting offers to go elsewhere. His home and studio are located at Short Pump, at the city's outskirts. He works there tirelessly, in the tradition of the great artist-illustrators. Those whom he regards as the best of the school are Howard Pyle, N. C. Wyeth, Norman Rockwell, and Ludwig Holwein of Germany. Although less famous than they, Jack Woodson is worthy to be mentioned in this select company.

His appearance, however, is far from that of the typical stereotype of the "artist." He does not wear his hair long—in fact, his cranium is almost devoid of hair. One might suspect that he would compensate for this with a walrus mustache, but no; his upper lip is clean-shaven. Furthermore, the Woodson cheeks are not adorned with sideburns, neither is the Woodson chin festooned with luxuriant whiskers. The fact is that he would be taken for a typical businessman, a stockbroker or insurance salesman, regular in attendance at Kiwanis. Oh well. It is Woodson's paintbrush, not his hairbrush, that matters.

The present volume is the first selection of his paintings to be published between book covers. It is sponsored by the United States Historical Society of Richmond, which has collaborated with him for decades and takes pride in the high quality of his work. The text by William L. Tazewell puts his career in perspective and provides many insights into his philosophy and his modus operandi.

DOWN TO THE SEA
WITH
JACK WOODSON

Jack Woodson has been going down to the sea since he was a boy, spending his summers by the seashore. Get him to talking, which is easy enough, and he keeps getting his conversational feet wet.

He remembers taking off for his aunt's beach house at Ocean View in Norfolk, Virginia, "as soon as school was out" each year. When he got a little older, he says, "My cousins and I wound up taking fishing parties out. In those days it wasn't anything at all to see four-masted schooners, and I was fascinated by all the activity down there. You could see battleships and freighters, particularly the Hog Islanders that were built during the First World War, and there were always a lot of small craft in the water."

When he was a young man, Jack began building boats himself. "I was in my twenties then," he recalls. "We built a 20-foot sloop, and then we built a 22-foot cabin cruiser. I had some friends who knew something about it, but it really was hard work." He learned to sail in a boat that he built himself, "the last one that a friend of mind and I built together. We built her to plans from *Popular Mechanics* and she was a wonderfully running small boat. I've been out of sight of land in her many times, and sometimes you do start to wonder whether that No. 4 frame is going to hold. . . .

"I spent a lot of time around the commercial marine railways gathering material and absorbing the atmosphere. At the time

NIGER

NEBEDFORD...

Whaler _Niger_   _12″ x 18″ serigraph_

C-2 Cargo Vessel   *40″ × 72″ oil on mounted canvas*

Clipper Ship *Neptune's Car*   *40″ × 72″ oil on mounted canvas*

Clipper Ship *Flying Cloud*   *40″ × 72″ oil on mounted canvas*

Whaler *Charles Morgan*
opaque watercolor

Steam barkentine *Bear* *opaque watercolor*

Old Dominion Line Steamboat *Luray*   *40" × 72" oil on mounted canvas*

Mississippi Steamboat *Gordon Greene*
30″ × 40″ oil on canvas

Chinese Junk *30″ × 40″ oil on canvas*

Chesapeake Bay Bugeyes
40" × 72" oil on mounted canvas

H.M.S. *Bounty* at Pitcairn Island
30" × 40" oil on canvas

"The Battle of the Capes," 1781   *30″ × 40″ oil on canvas*

my friend and I owned a 30-foot Chris Craft, which twice a year had to be hauled out to have the bottom cleaned and repainted with copper. In those days there were very few marinas as we know them today. The only way to haul out was on a commercial railway, and this usually meant being on the railway at the same time as perhaps a large workboat.

"On one occasion we were hauled out behind a large trawler whose crew was hosing down the hull. We were preparing to paint our hull bottom, and as a starter I began to paint a guide line along the side. I was using a one-inch brush, and though the line was a little shaky I thought I was doing pretty well. Some of the trawler's crew stopped to watch me and I glowed inwardly, knowing they must be envious of such a display of dexterity.

"I finally managed to finish the 30 feet of wobbly line and stood back awaiting the applause I was sure would follow. Instead, one of my audience bent over and picked up a large well-worn brush that was lying on the ground.

"'Guess I'd better get mine done,' he said.

"He slopped the big brush around in the bucket of paint and brushed off the excess on the rim. Walking up to the hull, he took a quick sight fore and aft. Then chunking the big brush against the hull, he began to walk, painting the line as he moved. Standing behind him I saw him paint an incredibly straight edge, no humps, no bumps, just smooth.

"I took my expensive one-inch brush, cleaned it out, and learned a lesson. The brush he was using, far from being a discard, had been cut at an angle much like what is called a sword striper, capable of carrying a good deal of color yet able to cut a sharp edge. In the hands of an experienced waterman it was an unbeatable combination.

"The crew did have the courtesy not to laugh at my effort, although I thought I detected a few grins."

He pauses, and returns to dry land and his listener. "Anyway, I became interested in why ships looked the way they did, and I had a chance to see some of them under sailing conditions, and then I started building ship models. That's where you really learn your ships.

"In fact, most of the European painters usually worked from

Three ship models: C-2 cargo vessel (top left), Mississippi River steamboat
Betsy Ann (bottom left), and steam barkentine *Bear* (right)

models," explains Jack, who is a born teacher as well as a natural storyteller. "I'm talking about the Dutch painters particularly, who to me are the epitome of maritime painters. Those people didn't guess at what they were doing. The worst thing you can do in painting a ship is to guess. If you guess, you'll get it wrong. . . ."

The first model Jack built was one of the *Preston*, a prototype four-piper destroyer of First World War vintage. "She was a long, narrow, skinny vessel that would beat you to death, but fast for the day," he recalls. "Of course, you built a model from scratch then; there were no plastic kits, and very few parts available to save time." He found plans for the *Preston* in *Popular Science*, Jack remembers, "and I was fascinated by the lines of the ship. It was rakish-looking, it had those four stacks, the torpedo tubes were in gangs of three and they would turn, and mine all turned too.

"One of the tricks in model-building is finding something, anything, that was never intended for what you want to use it for, but all of a sudden you can make it work." He is off on another story, about the time he went into a department store to buy nylon netting so he could stretch it on stanchions, spray it with white lacquer, and—lo and behold!—have railing of just the right scale on his model of the *Bear*. (The *Bear* was a barkentine built in Scotland as a sealing ship in 1874 and later purchased by the United States for Arctic service. After she was retired from the Coast Guard in 1929, she was reconditioned and used by Admiral Richard E. Byrd on his Antarctic expeditions. The *Bear* finally sank in a storm off Nova Scotia in 1963.) After the baffled saleslady in the nylon netting story gives Jack a sample, the anecdote ends in sudden triumph: "You can see it on the model on the shelf up there. It made a beautiful railing. . . ."

From the time the Mariners' Museum in Newport News, Virginia, was opened in 1930, Jack Woodson was fascinated with it. He became friendly with Bob Fee, who headed its model shop; Bob Burgess, the curator; John Lockhead, the librarian; and August Crabtree, the master modelmaker, whose work Jack describes as "pure genius." All four had an influence on his work. What impressed him most was their professionalism. "I never dreamed in those early days that someday my paintings and my

Hampton Roads Tugboat   *rough sketch for painting*

American Whaler *Wanderer*   *40" × 72" oil on mounted canvas*

"Sunday Morning," typical Chesapeake Bay craft   *30″ × 40″ oil on canvas*

President Reagan accepting presentation of Woodson painting
"Washington Fires First Shot," Williamsburg, Va., 1981

Dutch Yacht
16" × 20" opaque watercolor

"Old Ironsides"
stained glass

"Painting the Figurehead"
30″ × 40″ oil on canvas

"The Pilothouse Eagle,"
ornament being carved
for roof of tugboat
Dorothy

James River Steamboat *Pocahontas*
opaque watercolor

Sailor   *12" × 14" opaque watercolor*

Thomas Point Light *11″ × 14″ watercolor*

U.S.S. *Enterprise* **and tugboat, Christmas card for U.S. Navy** *10″ × 14″ opaque watercolor*

"Tramp Steamer in Squall"   *30″ × 40″ oil on canvas*

Mississippi steamboat *scratchboard*

ship models would be exhibited there in one of the most important marine museums in the world."

He once painted a picture of the steamboat *Pocahontas* on her Norfolk-to-Richmond run up the James River, and he remembers receiving a telephone call from Burgess after the painting was reproduced. Burgess said the painting was "pretty good," but the band around the stack should have been buff, not grey. "I had based my picture on black-and-white photographs of the long-gone *Pocahontas* and guessed at the color of the stack," admits Jack. "It doesn't ever pay to guess."

Woodson is meticulous in research, realistic in style. For instance, when he did a large painting of a C-2 cargo vessel, he built a model of the ship, working from the big builder's model in the Mariners' Museum and technical data that he obtained there. He decided to depict the vessel in Hampton Roads on a cloudy night, with Channel Marker Number 6 off her starboard bow. Such a painting, with details faithful to a large and a small working model while at the same time the ship is placed in an appropriate setting, demands a thorough knowledge of both the painter's and the seafarer's techniques. It is typical of Jack Woodson.

One of the most colorful sea stories Jack tells is about the time when he went along on an accompanying tug as a guest on the shakedown voyage of the *Susan Constant*, one of three replica vessels built in 1957 to commemorate the 350th anniversary of the founding of Jamestown. "The Coast Guard was sailing the ship, and we got off the Capes and passed a Greek freighter. The funny part about it was that a lot of the crew on board were wearing costumes of the period, and we were flying the British flag. The freighter's crew didn't have the slightest idea what it was all about. All of a sudden, they encountered an Elizabethan ship, with a costumed crew, sailing under a British flag—and we sailed right on by them. Everybody on the freighter must have thought it was the Flying Dutchman!"

Jack also made numerous trips to the Naval Academy at Annapolis. The museum there displays a collection of large Admiralty ship models that are a gold mine of information on ship construction of the age of sail. They were built in England and collected by Charles Sergison, who served subsequently to Sam-

Chesapeake Bay skipjack *pen drawing*

uel Pepys in the Office of Clerk of the Acts about 1690. They were purchased by Henry Huddleston Rogers from the Sergison heirs and presented, along with a number of other models, to the United States Naval Academy. According to Jack, "There was quite an uproar in England when news of the change of mooring became known."

"Among other models in the Naval Academy collection is an excellent one of Admiral de Grasse's flagship *Ville de Paris.* I used this model as the basis for the painting 'Battle of the Capes.' I have also used the Academy's model of the whaleship *Niger* in several drawings and paintings."

If Jack Woodson's stories tend to make him sound like the An-

Naval cannon and 1812 brig   *pen, pencil drawings*

cient Mariner now and then, he is not himself an old salt. He has spent his life painting pictures. If you cut Jack Woodson he would not bleed salt water or seaspray, but alizarine crimson or ultramarine pigment. Although best known for his paintings of ships, he is not exclusively a maritime painter. He has earned a comfortable living over many years by painting pictures that customers wanted. It has been a good life, and Jack would not have had it any different. He has done just what he wanted, and few have the privilege of saying that.

Several of his marine paintings are in the permanent collection of the Mariners' Museum, and others are in the Portsmouth Naval Museum. His ship models and paintings have been exhibited at both the Mariners' Museum and the Smithsonian Institution, and one of his portraits of Admiral Richard Byrd graces the wardroom of the guided missile cruiser U.S.S. *Virginia.* Two paintings that he did originally for the United States Historical Society were acquired by the Commonwealth of Virginia as the gifts of the state to Presidents Reagan and Mitterrand to commemorate the Bicentennial of the Battle of Yorktown in 1981. "The Battle of the Capes," depicting a French victory in Chesapeake Bay, was presented to President Mitterrand; President Reagan was given a painting of Washington firing the first shot at the siege of Yorktown.

"Being involved in a diversity of painting projects has enabled me to meet and work with many interesting and talented people," Jack says. "The presentation of the presidential paintings was certainly one of the highlights of my life. It took place at a formal dinner in Williamsburg, with Governor Dalton, the governors of most of the other states, Cabinet members, and foreign dignitaries. Egypt's President Sadat had just been assassinated, and security was unbelievably tight. But when President and Mrs. Reagan and President and Mme. Mitterrand entered the room and the Navy Band played the American and French national anthems, it lifted you right out of your seat. It was an unforgettable evening for me."

Jack looks up at a framed reproduction of his painting of the Battle of Yorktown, which is hanging on the study wall, and is reminded of a story. He points to the picture, which portrays Washington himself, who had sighted the cannon, watching the

Design for figurehead
pencil drawing

22

first shot being fired. "There's an artillery observer up on the parapet, with a telescope, looking toward Yorktown, and I always thought a good title would be '*It's in the river, George!*'"

Another favorite story is about the time when Robert Burgess, curator of the Mariners' Museum, commissioned Jack to do a painting of the Mississippi steamboat *Gordon Greene*.

"It was a large picture loaded with detail. The steamboat had experienced a number of structural changes during its lifetime, but my instructions were to do a generic *Gordon Greene* and I did what I could with the information I had. I completed the painting and delivered it to the museum director, Admiral Sylvester. The Admiral, a retired submariner, sat behind his desk and silently studied the picture for what seemed an eternity. He broke the silence with, 'You ever been in Louisiana?'

"'Well, ah, no, sir.' I wondered how he knew.

"'Thought so,' he went on, not helping any.

"'How do you know, Admiral?'

"He pointed to some figures I had painted in the foreground. 'You see those men there?'

"'Yes, sir.'

"'You see that man helping the other one load the jon boat?'

"'Yes, sir.'

"'Well, they'd never do that in Louisiana.'"

Another painting that Woodson did for the Mariners' Museum was of the figurehead from the ship *Belle of Oregon*. Painted from the original figurehead in the Museum's collection, it showed the figurehead in the foreground and a sailing ship of the period in the background. The painting was reproduced a number of times, once on the cover of the *United States Naval Institute Proceedings*. Another magazine that reproduced the picture described it as a photograph of the actual figurehead taken in front of a painting. "I always tried to paint realistically, but I didn't know whether to be flattered or not," Woodson says.

"I was asked to prepare some art involving the then-new aircraft carrier *Enterprise*," he recalls. "I was quite excited when I was invited to lunch on board with the captain. This was the first nuclear-powered aircraft carrier, the largest ship in the world and the ultimate in the state of the art. I could hardly wait to go aboard. She was at the Norfolk Naval Base for some minor work, and so was close to home.

"I arrived alongside at the appointed time and was greeted on board by the officer of the deck, complete with white gloves and brass telescope. He in turn introduced me to Commander Killeen, who because of the immense size of the ship could only give me a quick tour before it was time for lunch.

"In most ships, below decks is a confusing array of passageways, watertight doors, and miles and miles of pipes, cables, and conduits. The *Enterprise* certainly had her share. Somewhere in this maze Killeen found the wardroom, which surprisingly somewhat resembled a night club, with the exception, of course, of the pipe and conduit tangles overhead.

"We were seated at a long table, at places indicated by place cards which carried a color photo of the ship and the name of the guest. (I still have mine.) I was seated directly opposite Captain Michaelis, skipper of the *Enterprise.* As I sat there making small talk with the brass, I kept wondering what would be served for lunch. Pheasant under glass, caviar, some gourmet delight? It would have to be something extraordinary indeed.

"The mess boys began serving and I planned to follow whatever the captain did. What they were serving looked suspiciously like hot dogs, but I knew it just couldn't be. The captain stuck his fork in one, placed it on his plate and asked me to pass the mustard. I couldn't believe it! It *was* hot dogs, and close behind them came the beans. Franks and beans! My idols had feet of clay.

"I was told later that when a ship is in home port, most of the officers eat ashore and those remaining eat whatever is available in the galley. I never told my friends, but I guess I'll have to go to sea if I ever want pheasant under glass."

John Waddie Woodson was born in Richmond, Virginia, on January 23, 1913. His father worked in a furniture store; his mother had previously taught school. He can trace the family tree back to Dr. John Woodson, who with his wife, Sarah, sailed on the ship *George* to the colony at Jamestown in the seventeenth century. Dr. Woodson was killed by raiding Indians as he tried to reach his home just outside the fort. During the attack Mrs. Woodson hid her two boys, one in a hole under the floor

Elizabethan soldier
pen drawing

25

where potatoes were stored and the other under a large tub. Jack says he doesn't know whether he is descended from the "potato-hole" Woodsons or the "tub" Woodsons.

An early influence on Jack Woodson was his father, "who was a fairly good amateur draftsman, though he worked for a furniture store. He'd taken a correspondence course from the old International Schools, back in the late 'nineties, I guess. If I could get my father to sit down and draw me some birds, I thought that was the greatest thing in the world. He'd studied penmanship, and in those days penmanship was a real art. There were books of birds drawn with a pen with all the flourishes, and there was one page of Jesus drawn with one line, in a circle, the line varying in thickness. They were masterpieces of pen work.

"My father did a lot of that, so I was fascinated with the instruments, and I was able to use drafting instruments before I even went to school. My folks were smart; they never pushed me. They encouraged me, but they never said, 'This is what you are going to do.' I don't think that works."

Jack "wanted to draw pictures" from the time that he was a small boy—"and I mean small." He was given art lessons after school. "I'd go to school up till three o'clock, and then from three to five I'd go to a private class with some other kids. There was nowhere else to go, and the teacher was wonderful.

"She had a sister in Williamsburg who owned a rental library, the first one I'd ever heard of, right behind the court house. This was in the 1920s, before Rockefeller ever found Williamsburg, and at that time about the only thing worth looking at was the Powder Magazine, which had grown up with ivy all around it. So I'd ride down to Williamsburg and she'd dump me out and I'd take a little sketch pad and make sketches. She'd take them and put mats around them and display them in the library. Well, the first thing I knew, somebody bought one for three dollars.

"I couldn't believe that. I said, this is ridiculous! Three dollars was a lot of money in those days; I'd cut all the grass in the neighborhood for thirty cents. That's when I found out people would pay me to draw a picture. The other thing I discovered was that they were willing to do it *only* if it was something they wanted, like the old Powder Magazine. I guess it did influence me, because I saw there could be a market for what you were

Covered wagon and oxen   *pen drawing*

Guilford Courthouse North Carolina March 15, 1781

Jack Woodson

Revolutionary War soldier, Guilford Courthouse   *pen drawing*

"Goin' Fishing," Jack Woodson's first published
drawing (1928)

doing, but only if it was something that somebody else wanted.
So I'm still doing that today."

Of course, Jack still was "fighting the stuff, because I didn't
know how to draw it. Then I found out there were people who
could tell me. I had some wonderful teachers who gave me a
background that was priceless, you couldn't buy it today, in perspective, composition, color systems, technical things. . . . I
drew a flax wheel, I must have made two hundred drawings of
that flax wheel, trying to understand the principles of perspective. A flax wheel goes in six different directions at the same
time. It's on three legs, the base sits at an angle, you have an
ellipse in the wheel, the supports to the wheel run at an angle to

Boeing P-12, Woodson's first commercial project

"The Oregon Trail," art for musket patchbox engraving   *pen drawing*

nothing, it's in about six different picture planes, and to try to make that flax wheel look like it was sitting on the floor was a nightmare.

"That was the thing. I got so fascinated with perspective that I would distort it just for fun, because I knew what to do with it. It was like discovering the Rosetta Stone. I had the knowledge, I knew where the vanishing points were supposed to be, I knew where the aesthetic center in the composition was. It's easy. Anybody with average intelligence can understand it, but so many people don't take the trouble."

H. L. Mencken once wrote a celebrated diatribe dismissing the entire South as "the Sahara of the Bozart." Although the essay offended local pride and met with indignant responses all across

Dixie, what Mencken said was largely true. In the capital of the Confederacy, where young Jack Woodson was growing up, the Virginia Museum of Fine Arts had not yet been built. Woodson's Louvre would be the commercial engraving houses in Richmond.

When he was in high school, he worked on the annual, the newspaper, and other publications. This experience "was priceless because it gave me a chance to get into the engraving houses and gave me a background in reproduction that still pays off." Occasionally he would go to Washington, D.C., where a cousin was studying at the Corcoran Gallery, "but even then they were into the avant-garde stuff, and that didn't interest me. If I wanted to draw a tiger, I wanted it to look like a tiger. . . .

"You had your heroes, and these people did pretty well. For example, I used to watch Day Lowry. He worked for the Everett Waddey Company and he'd let me come down to his studio. He had a rug on the floor and an easel: that was heaven, it was something to shoot for. So I went to every class I could get into, I had three years of a life class, and I began to pick things up, little jobs, and kept pretty busy."

Jack was doing "saleable stuff" while he was in high school. "Gosh, I did everything from biscuits on flour bags to I don't know what. I did a lot for the old Milhiser Bag Company; they made bags for flour and baking powder. I could really draw hot rolls; I was a great pancake painter.

"I spent one summer working for the Cohen Department Store lettering show cards: white cards, lettered in black ink with 'Speedball' pens. Whenever I'd finish one batch of cards there would be another to do. My show card efforts were certainly no award winners, but here again it all contributed to my general fund of usable skills."

When he graduated from John Marshall High School in 1930, college was out of the question. He didn't care about "classic Greek or trigonometry or any of the rest," and he already knew what he wanted to do with his life. But it was right at the beginning of the Depression, and he couldn't find anybody who would pay him to draw pictures. So he got a job at the DuPont factory near Richmond—and hated it. He made thirteen dollars a week, and he used what little money he could spare to buy art supplies.

"The only art supply house in Richmond was down on Main

"Washington Fires the First Shot at Yorktown" *30″ × 40″ oil on canvas*

Map of Colonial Yorktown
30″ × 40″ opaque watercolor

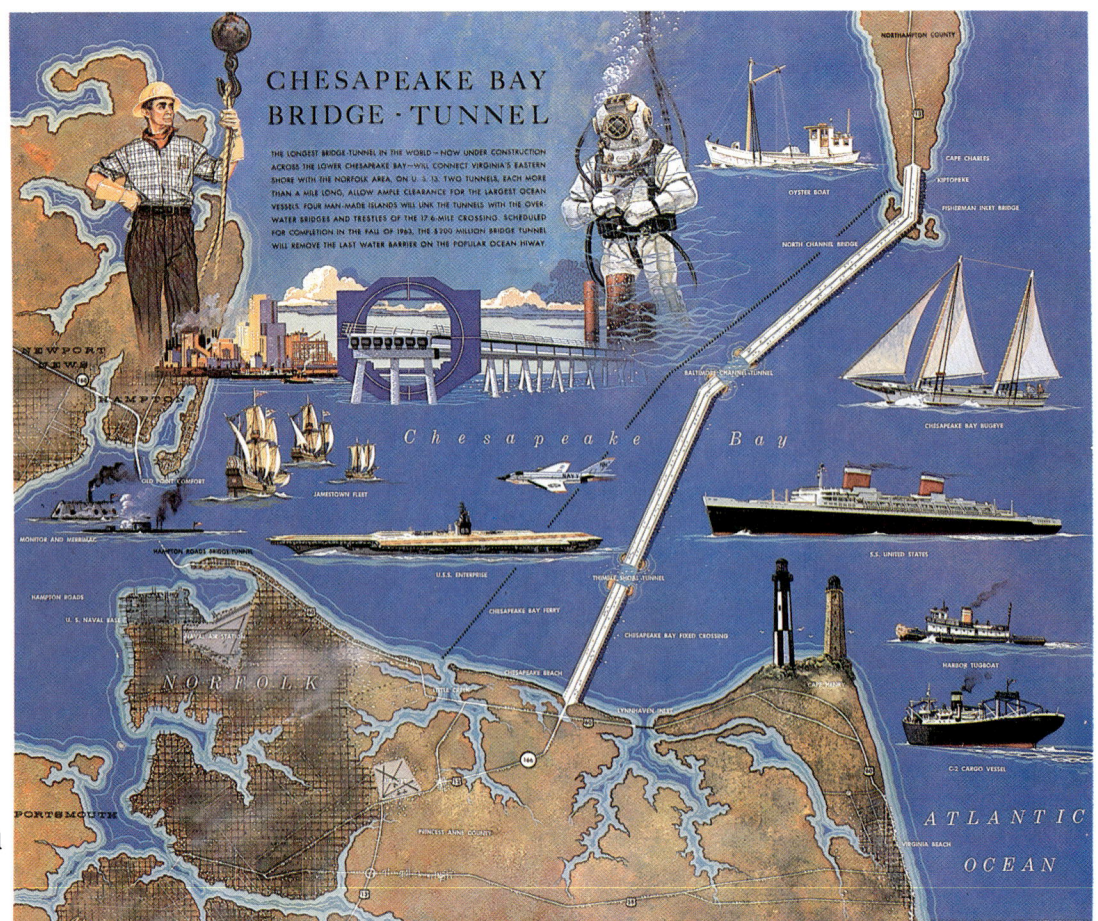

Chesapeake Bay Bridge-Tunnel
24″ × 30″ opaque watercolor

Benjamin Franklin   *16″ × 20″ opaque watercolor*

Lafayette   *16″ × 20″ opaque watercolor*

Season's Greetings *Virginia Trust Company* Richmond, Virginia

James River and Kanawha Canal Boat
opaque watercolor

Derringer *opaque watercolor*

"Johnny Reb and Billy Yank"   *10″ × 15″ oil on canvas*

Buffalo Bill series, reproduced on porcelain: Pony Express, Buffalo hunter, Annie Oakley, Sitting Bull

Thaddeus S. C. Lowe's Civil War balloon *Intrepid*, Fair Oaks,
Virginia, 1862

"Out of the Sun," World War I gunner   *16″ × 20″ opaque watercolor*

"Tomorrow the Moon,"
Curtiss JN-4 (Jenny)
20" × 30" oil on canvas

"Aw, C'mon," magazine advertisement
12" × 18" opaque watercolor

Robert E. Lee, art for engraving

World War I doughboy   *pen drawing*

Street, and I went in there one day and saw a little sign sitting on the counter. It said:

```
ART LESSONS
J. P. Derrenberger
Loew's Theater
```

Holy mackerel, for me that was like the Second Coming. I couldn't wait. I went up and met Jack Derrenberger. He'd just come from the West Coast, he'd worked for the Million Dollar Theater in Los Angeles, he'd worked in Texas, he'd worked in Atlanta, he'd worked in all these big houses. He did all the posters, the newspaper ads, everything that went with the theater business.

"He was going to give lessons for a dollar a night, with materials supplied by an unsuspecting Loew's Theater. I didn't have a dollar. Nobody had any money, but we scrounged around at home and I went. There were about six or eight of us, and it was the damnedest art class that ever existed. But I learned a lot from him. I'd never seen anybody who used pastel like he did; I'd never seen anybody who handled a brush the way he did, which is the way I still do; I'd never seen anybody who did a lot of things he did. Well, the class dwindled down until I was the only one left. Derrenberger was up to his ears in work—this was the Depression, but I've never seen a slump in what I was doing—and he couldn't handle it all, so he called me up at home and talked to my mother. It's hard to describe how I felt when I found out I had the chance to go to work as an artist in Loew's Theater.

"I went down to the factory the next day and told them I was quitting. They were horrified; I hadn't given them two weeks' notice. I said, 'No, I can't, I'm quitting today. I'm going to be an artist.' So I went with Jack. The first picture I ever worked on was called *Night Flight*, with John and Lionel Barrymore, and I worked myself to death down there. Many a night we'd work until two or three A.M. But honestly, I didn't like to come home at night. I couldn't wait to get back there. It was fascinating."

Woodson at Loew's Theater, 1935, painting poster of W. C. Fields in "David Copperfield"

Loew's Theater, newspaper art, redrawn from original by Elmo Jones

Being involved in show business in the 'thirties was wonderful. "It was another world for me," Jack remembers. "In those days a deluxe theater like Loew's would have its own art department. I did newspaper ads, stuff for magazines, and the posters. I was doing the big three-sheet posters. They were only good for a week, then they were thrown away. Today these originals are collector's items and are bought at high prices by theater buffs. We must have thrown away a fortune!

"I'd do one poster a day—the last one I did was for *Mrs. Miniver.* It was the greatest training I could have had. You learned all about deadlines and discipline. You learned about working fast. You had to. Like it or not, you had to do it."

It was one of the most enjoyable periods in Jack's life. He joined the International Association of Theatrical Stage Employees "because I did a lot of stage sets, and you couldn't set foot on stage or do anything around the theater if you didn't belong to the union. But there was no local chapter, so we were members of Local Number 1018 of the Plasterers, Painters, and Paperhangers, A.F.L. We never went to any meetings. We just paid our dues and they left us alone."

He came to know a lot of show people, such as the magician Harry Blackstone and the bandleader Fred Waring. He was commissioned to do portraits by Marie McDonald, the movie star who was called "The Body," and also by Walter Brennan, in his role as Judge Roy Bean, "the law west of the Pecos."

The shop was located underneath the Loew's stage, and Jack remembers working with the Fred Waring orchestra rehearsing in the same room. "I played ping-pong with him many a time; I knew all of those people. Seeing the show, that was part of it. Not only did you see them, you heard them all day because we were under the stage. We knew all the Marx Brothers' lines. I still do. I don't know how we got any work done. It was quite a time."

Before the war came, the three of them—Jack Derrenberger, Jack Woodson, and Mike Kimmel, who did lettering—moved out of the theater and into new quarters at Seventh and Main Streets. There were almost no advertising agencies in Richmond then, and Jack and the others were taking on considerable outside work. "People say, 'How did they find you?' That's easy. If you've

Harry Blackstone *8″ × 10″ crayon*

"Mademoiselle from Armentieres"   *pen drawing*

got your name on the picture, they'll find you. They'll track you down. The 'thirties, they were priceless. It was all a big fun time, and I learned a lot, too."

Then the war came along. Jack tried to volunteer for the Navy V-12 program, but was turned down. "So I started doing bond posters. I did a lot of USO stuff. The ridiculous thing was they started sending classes from Fort Lee over for me to teach. They'd send a busload over and I'd teach them how to use drafting instruments. It was illogical. I could have been doing that in uniform, but the Army wouldn't take me. I was still cranking out stuff all during the war, and I continued doing it."

At about this time Jack was first introduced to Iris Snead by a friend, a painter, who arranged a blind date. When they got home Jack invited Iris to see *The Student Prince* a couple of days later, and pretty soon they were dating steadily.

"There were so many things he was interested in, so many things he could do. Every time I would see him it was a surprise," Iris says. "Of course, my mother thought Jack was The

World War II infantryman with carbine   *crayon*

One, and I guess we went together for a couple of years." They were married at the First Baptist Church on June 25, 1943.

"It was real funny," Iris says. "We were just going to go into the office and get married. So we went to talk to Dr. Theodore Adams, our minister. My mother went, and my aunt, and my best friend, and there were Jack's mother and father and some of his family. The church was having Vacation Bible School at the time, and while we were in the office there was a knock on the door. It was Dr. Adam's wife, and she was very apologetic, but the Vacation Bible School children were collecting for the lepers. They thought it would be pretty good if they got twenty-five dollars, and if they got fifty dollars that would be really good, and if they got seventy-five that would be grand, but if they got a hundred that would be a miracle. They lacked fifty cents of having a hundred dollars, so she'd come to get it from him. After she went out, Dr. Adams turned to Jack and said, 'Now that's what husbands are for—to make miracles come true.'"

"Jack told me when we got married, 'Well, I don't guess we'll ever have any money, but it will be interesting,'" Iris says. "And it has been interesting."

"Years ago I thought that when I got out of high school I would go somewhere to study art, but then Daddy was killed [he was a policeman, shot by a criminal] and that was the end of that. Then, when I met Jack, I realized I couldn't carry his brushes. After we got married my mother said, "You'll have to stop talking about Jack like that; people will think you're bragging. Nobody could be as good as you think he is.'

"They say opposites attract," Iris says, "and that's the truth with us. It may have been because Daddy was killed and I had to go to work and make a living, so I didn't have much time for playing. Now we've been married for so long, we don't even have to talk to each other to know what the other's thinking.

"Jack always had a studio. He always felt like he had to get in the automobile and go to work, just like everybody else, but he always had a studio at home, too."

At first he was working in a big studio on Clay Street, where he had all the room he wanted. "It was a monstrous place, almost as big as this house, with a big darkroom and top-level lighting," he says. "I could do a thirty-foot mural in there without

John Marshall House, drawing for John Marshall High School yearbook, 1930 *pencil*

Judge William Spain, Frank Shepperson, and Woodson with original painting, "Tomorrow the Moon"

any problem." After they moved out to Short Pump, now a suburb of Richmond, Jack built himself a separate studio outside where he could keep on painting. But he had an immediate problem: "I said to Iris, 'This is terrible. I tell you goodbye in the morning and go out there, and I don't feel like I've gone to work.' So I started getting in the car and driving around the block. I'd come back, and then I'd be at work. That made me feel normal."

"Normal" is an adjective that attaches easily to Jack Woodson. He defies every popular stereotype of the Artist. In instinct and life style, he is resolutely un-Bohemian. You cannot imagine him in a loft in SoHo. Abstraction, alienation, the anti-hero, the concepts that are fashionably modern, are not for Jack Woodson, who refers jokingly to himself as "the Lawrence Welk of the graphic arts." His pictures are plain-spoken, practical, unambiguous. Look at any picture painted by Jack Woodson and you might suspect that his muse has a degree in engineering, or perhaps naval architecture. You know that what he paints runs, ticks, works.

Like anybody who came of age during the Depression, Jack Woodson is a child of that time. Few families, including his, had any money to spare then. The child of economic insecurity is always insecure somewhere in his soul, whatever his later success. This feeling has very little to do with economic reality.

The fact is that Jack has been a good provider, as is evident from his comfortable Williamsburg-style colonial home in Short Pump. (The name, which always amuses strangers, has an honorable pedigree. There once was a busy colonial tavern on the old Three Chopt Road west of Richmond, about halfway to Gum Spring. The tavern's well was located near the porch, and when it was enlarged the new porch protruded so that it was difficult to get a full stroke on the old pump handle. Since it was easier to shorten the handle of the pump than to dig a new well, the hostelry soon was known as "the tavern with the short pump handle," inevitably shortened in time to Short Pump.)

The decor of the Woodson house is a homey mix of Jack's and Iris's hobbies, a blend of the comfortable and the practical, with enough odds and ends that Jack has squirreled away over the years to keep the place from appearing conventionally suburban. The entry hall opens into a large room with a cathedral ceiling and transverse beams. It has a Steinway grand piano and a Hammond organ, with its speakers recessed into the ceiling. (Iris plays the piano. Jack says that he "only plays for his own amazement" and adds that he "never plays for friends if they can help it.") Among the furnishings are baroque mirrors and Spanish chairs and tables that were rescued and refinished when the old Loew's Theater was renovated.

There are a number of Jack's paintings on the wall—a portrait of Iris, another of the grandchildren, maritime pictures, a painting of the windmill at Williamsburg. Jack's library reflects his

Section of Woodson's storeroom of artifacts

interest in matters nautical, as do many objects displayed in glass showcases or scattered on shelves—a diving helmet, ship's lanterns, ship models, mock pieces-of-eight and the real thing, as well as an array of armaments ancient and modern. One wall is filled with photographs that commemorate moments in Jack's career as a painter: Admiral Byrd, Billy Graham, Harold Peterson, Vincent Price, Norman Rockwell, President Reagan and President Mitterrand.

But not until Jack leads his visitor into his studio—his "Little House on the Prairie," as he calls it—is the painter really revealed. His studio is a garage-sized outbuilding (it measures 10 feet by 16 feet) with a large north-light window. It is filled with easels and drawing tables, brushes and paints, photography

BAT MASTERSON

JESSE JAMES

DOC HOLLIDAY

JACK WOODSON

Law of the Old West   *pen drawing*

Drawing for Washington musket engraving

equipment, file cabinets containing a lifetime's hoard of clippings and photographs indexed by subject, books ranked on shelves, and the props for past, present, and yet-to-be painted pictures—costume hats on pegs, firearms, and more ship models. The miscellany of objects is a mix of security blanket, talismans, and tools of the trade: the clutter of a craftsman's work place.

When he goes about painting a picture, he starts with a series of pencil sketches. The first will be little more than doodles, quick sketches to see how an idea looks on paper. As the composition and content of the picture start to shape themselves in his mind, the sketches become more tangible. The first rough sketches yield to a comprehensive color layout, smaller than the finished painting will be but done to scale. Once he is satisfied with the composition, he makes a detailed drawing in pencil on a canvas that he has already prepared. He uses models for the figures in the painting and any props that are pertinent to the subject.

By preparing the subject so thoroughly he guarantees that he will meet with few surprises when he actually begins to paint. The compositional problems are solved, and there will be few distractions in the actual process of putting paint on the canvas, following his own sketch in the time-honored way.

After the pencil sketch has been sprayed with retouch var-

"Duty, Honor, Country,"
U.S. Military Academy, West Point
26″ × 30″ oil on canvas

Space Shuttle
20″ × 30″ air brush

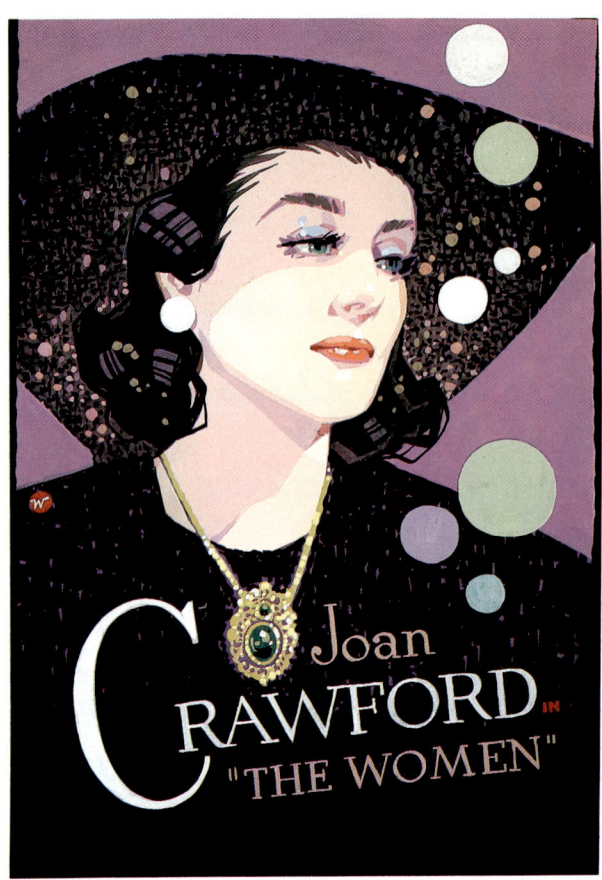

Theater Posters *31″ × 57″ oil on wallboard*

Snowy Egret   *20" × 30" acrylic on board*

World Missions mural, seven panels
72″ × 30′ oil on mounted canvas

Self-portrait, magazine cover   *16″ × 20″ oil on canvas*

Antarctic   *12″ × 16″ opaque watercolor*

"The Emperor's Nightingale,"
painting for reproduction on porcelain
14″ diam. opaque watercolor

"Huck Finn"
18″ × 24″ oil on canvas

Background and overlay for animated cartoon
original 9″ × 12″ opaque watercolor

"Hard Hat Diver"
30″ × 40″ oil on canvas

Henry VIII, design for playing card
16″ × 20″ opaque watercolor

Elizabeth I, design for playing card
16″ × 20″ opaque watercolor

nish to fix the image and has been allowed to dry, Woodson is ready to begin brushing a thin wash of burnt umber and turpentine over the entire picture. Again it is allowed to dry, and he begins the basic modeling, using Mars violet and turpentine. Working from dark to light, he applies additional colors to the picture, sometimes using a heavy impasto, sometimes "wet into wet," whatever the end effect requires of the painter's technique. The eye tells the hand what to do in order to bring the whole picture up. As in portrait painting, the final touch typically is the highlight on the nose.

Woodson uses Dr. Martin's, Luma and Winsor, and Newton water color, and opaque watercolor by Richart. His palette includes the following colors: alizarine crimson, vermilion, chrome yellow, lemon yellow, yellow ochre, burnt sienna, burnt umber, raw umber, chrome oxide green, ultramarine blue, cobalt blue, turquoise blue, Payne's grey, mars violet, and Permalba white. The oil painting surface is gesso primed canvas. For watercolor #100 crescent illustration board is used. Sable brushes, both round and flat, are used almost entirely. Mechanical equipment includes a Paasche AB airbrush, a 4 × 5 Graphic camera with Polaroid back, a 35mm Minolta, a 4 × 5 Omega Enlarger, and a Bausch and Lomb Opaque Projector.

Jack Woodson's two basic principles are *Get It Right* and *Do It on Time.* "When you're working as I do," he says, "when there are deadlines involved, you don't have the time to keep fooling around with what you're doing. The more you fool around with something that's beginning to go wrong, the worse it's going to get. You're better off to junk it and start over again."

Get It Right is a corollary to *Do It on Time,* insofar as the client must be satisfied and it takes time to correct wrong details or eliminate unwanted ones. But the notion that everything in a picture must be true-to-life is bone-deep in the character of Jack Woodson. He cares about the little things that testify to the painting's veracity, and he gets great satisfaction when he is complimented on details or the fact that he got the rigging right when he painted a ship.

As we have seen, he gets things right because he refuses to guess. Whenever he paints a figure, for instance, he works from a model—Iris has modeled for him often through the years—in

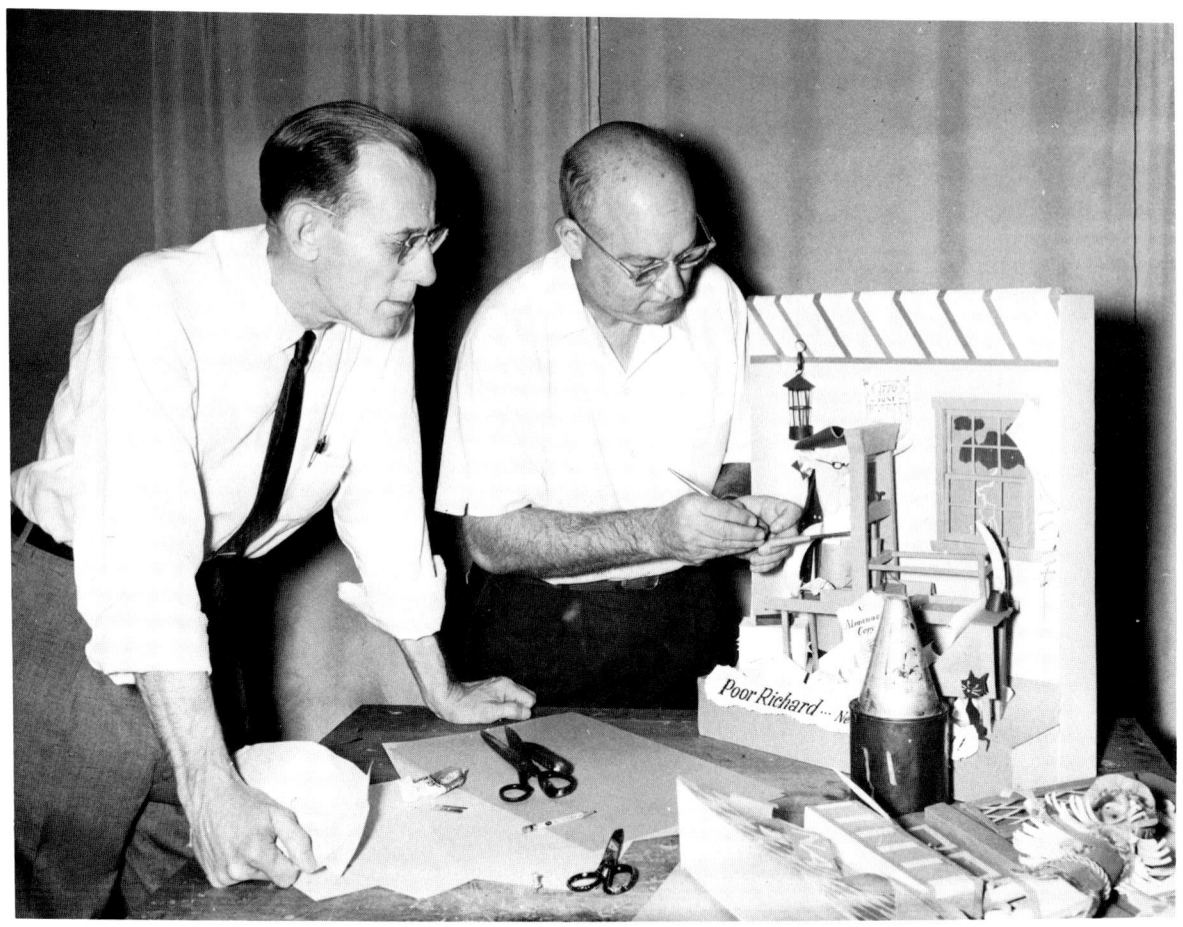

Assembling cutouts for a paper sculpture

order to be sure that the folds in the sleeve, say, are just right. If Jack puts something in his picture, you had better believe it belongs there, and he can tell you why.

"Some years ago," he says, "I did a painting for *Fortune* magazine, which is not exactly the place to hide anything, showing the first use of the McCormick reaper, in the Valley of Virginia. After the painting was published, the agency got a letter of complaint and called me up. In the background of the reaper I had painted a windmill. The person who complained said he had been born and raised on the farm next to the McCormicks', and there were never any windmills. The agency said, 'What about it?'

"I said, tell him this. If he'll come down to Richmond, I'll take him down in the basement of the old State Library where there's

Norman Rockwell   *9″ × 12″ crayon*

a museum nobody knows about except maybe the custodian and me, and there's a model of the McCormick reaper and there's also a model of the blacksmith shop where the McCormick reaper was built and the farmhouse there, and a lot of photographs showing windmills.

"There are still places in the Shenandoah Valley where there are footings for the windmills, I said, and tell your friend who says he was born and raised next to the McCormicks' that the reaper was never tested on the McCormick farm. The farm it was tested on was right next to the windmill I show. . . ."

Case closed.

Give Jack a historical or mechanical problem to solve when he is painting a picture, and he is like a boy with a new toy. He is a bear on detail, a demon for research. "I think the secret to education," he says, "is not being able to remember things, but knowing where to find them. Ask me to paint a picture of the Taj Mahal today, and I'll find out everything there is to know about the Taj Mahal before I begin.

"Iris says I have the greatest fund of useless knowledge she ever heard of—which is not always a blessing, to her way of thinking." They will be watching a program on television together when Jack takes off on some error he has spotted. "Last night we were watching *Columbus* for the second time"—Jack is talking—"and I've never seen so many errors in my life. The rigging was the sorriest-looking stuff, it looked like clothesline, and they used deadeyes, which didn't come in until after the Elizabethan period, and they showed a great big figurehead of Medusa on the *Santa Maria*. Ridiculous! People say, what difference does it make? It makes a lot of difference. For Pete's sake, they've got the ship wrong! How can I depend on what they have Isabella saying, when they've got the wrong ship?

"We're back to the importance of researching. When I start something, I won't say I don't make mistakes. Everybody makes mistakes. I won't bat 1.000, nobody does—but you try awfully hard, and if there's a mistake it isn't because you didn't try. There are always people who know the difference, and the last thing I want is a painting coming back with something wrong. . . ."

Iris Woodson offers a second view. "He can ruin movies on television," she says. "He'll sit there and start shaking his head.

"The Man with the Horn"   *photograph*

'Just don't tell me,' I say, 'I don't care.' He says, 'Well, at least they could have got it right. They didn't have telephones like that at that time.' 'Well, I don't care,' I say, 'it doesn't matter to me.' But he doesn't miss a thing.''

Woodson doesn't miss a thing because he is the old-fashioned sort who likes to know how things work. He has always loved to fool around with airplanes, he has built boats, he knows a lot about firearms. He is a natural tinkerer, a throwback to the generation who puttered about in garages and makeshift shops before doing-it-yourself was the vogue. It is a passion that shows in his work.

For all the joy he takes in painting, Woodson has never forgotten that it is his way of putting the daily bread on his table. "I'm a great bird-in-hander," he says. "I never took chances, I always played it safe. . . . What I depended on was people coming back—I'd do this, and then they'd want me to do another one like that, and another one like that. . . ."

Because he did his job well, he always had plenty of work. "To me, that has been the most amazing thing of all," Jack says. "I never had an agent, I never had a gallery. I could sell all my time, so there really was no reason for me to speculate. For instance, take that picture there on the wall—it's not the 'Mona Lisa' by any means, but the man paid me to paint that. Now I didn't particularly want to paint that piano-player, but he said that's what he wanted, so I painted him a piano-player.

If he had "speculated," Jack would get up in the morning "and I'd say, 'Gee, I don't know, today, I think I'll paint a rainy scene, looking up the street, with automobile headlights, and I'm going to do so-and-so. . . .' I'm going to paint that thing, and it's liable to sit there for two or three years. Who needs that?" Instead, he had a backlog of customers' orders, often as many as thirty at a time, and he was busy keeping up with all of that work. What he did was to go to his studio, stay there working, and then come home at night and keep on working.

"Everybody in this business," Iris remembers, "wants everything yesterday. In those days he worked all the time. We used to go to church on Sunday and come home afterwards, and he'd start working. He nearly always worked at night after he came home from his studio. He'd come home and have some dinner and then he'd go into the room he'd fixed up where he could work, and he'd be painting again. . . .

"The first vacation we ever took was after our daughter Pam was married. It was a beautiful place, Litchfield Beach. We stayed four days." Then Jack was back home, back at work.

He has produced so many pictures through the years, for so many people, that he has lost count of them. Even Iris, who handles the billing, does the books, sees to the files, and generally keeps track of things, cannot always remember. "At first," she says, "he'd always bring his latest work and show it to me, but he's turned out so much that I don't even get to see it all anymore."

Jack Woodson

"Snowed In" *pen drawing*

Among the clients for Jack's output have been a number of advertising agencies, large corporations, and publishers, as well as the people who have bought his pictures or commissioned him to paint portraits. He has also done animated films for NASA and the *National Geographic*, designed Christmas cards for the National Rifle Association and the U.S. Navy, made documentary motion pictures and commercials for television, painted art for porcelain and stained glass, designed and decorated three major restaurants, painted murals for the Baptist Foreign Mission Board and a corporate jet for the Ethyl Corporation, been commissioned to do paintings for the National Park Service, and illustrated dozens of books.

One of his happiest long-standing relationships is with Robert Kline and the United States Historical Society. An ex-newspaper reporter and Navy officer, Kline first met Jack Woodson on an assignment: a feature story on the first portrait that Jack was painting of Admiral Byrd. After Kline left the newspaper to go into public relations work, one of his first jobs was handling the publicity for the building of the Chesapeake Bay Bridge-Tunnel. He asked Woodson to paint a panoramic map of the crossing that gave people the first clear idea of what the mighty bridge-tunnel would look like. Later Jack also designed a large-scale model of the bridge-tunnel.

For the occasion of the bicentennial celebration of American independence, Woodson was commissioned by Kline to design a sword, which was to be fabricated by the Wilkinson Company, the English swordmakers, their first-ever American-designed sword. The blade was engraved, the guard had two gold eagles on laurel leaves of sterling silver, and the hilt was ornamented with a golden knot, three sapphires, and thirteen diamonds. The sword sold for $3,000, and the edition was limited to one thousand. The first of these swords was presented to President Gerald Ford, the second to the British Ambassador to the United States, and Jack has the third in Short Pump, Virginia.

Many other projects sponsored by the United States Historical Society have carried Jack's mark and style. He has been involved in designing replicas of firearms and knives, music boxes, commemorative plates, and a series of porcelain figurines of storybook characters, all offered for sale by the Society. He has

SHOTGUN

DEADLIEST WEAPON OF THE AMERICAN WEST

BY

JOSEPH E. DOCTOR

Book cover   *pen drawing*

Hispaniola Restaurant, Hampton, Virginia

also designed a number of annual Christmas plates and done the design work for a variety of stained glass plates and tableaux for the Society. Jack's work as a commercial designer has brought him commissions from Royal Copenhagen/Bing & Grondahl in Denmark; his "Christmas in Williamsburg," the first American plate they marketed, was highly successful.

Another project Jack remembers warmly was designing the Hispaniola Restaurant on the Hampton, Virginia, waterfront. Although the buildings have since been demolished, Hampton Roads residents remember the half-timbered frontage that was dominated by the rigging and stern of Long John Silver's brig, the complex containing a modern restaurant with 600 seats.

Merchant seaman   *photograph*

The concept came from the pages of Robert Louis Stevenson; the decor and design were Jack Woodson's. He did a dozen maritime paintings to hang in the restaurant and supervised all the details of its decoration, including the casting of an iron cannon for the foyer (it had to be test-fired to prove that it worked). A typically ingenious touch was disguising the condensers for the air-conditioning system as eighteenth-century barrels and packing crates, part of the brig's deck cargo.

The Hispaniola project was undertaken with Sam Carmine, who hired Woodson as a vice president of Carmine Foods to oversee the work. (That was the only prolonged period in his life when Jack was on anybody else's payroll.) Jack and Sam Carmine made several trips to Haiti to commission figureheads and carvings from native woodworkers, an adventure Jack remembers as the time "when I played Peter Lorre opposite Sam's Humphrey Bogart."

"Sam and I spent a lot of time on the waterfront at Port-au-Prince, Haiti, a bustling, steamy place where we had an opportunity to see close up the construction of some Caribbean small craft. These boats had basically beautiful lines and in the hands of skilled craftsmen would have been quite acceptable, but the combination of terrible material and lack of mechanical skills was a disaster.

"One boat owner with a smattering of English tried to interest me in accompanying him to Panama on his boat. He had a sloop-rigged 40-footer that seemed barely able to float. No engine, no compass, a foot of water in the bilge and no pump. Sharing this craft was the ever-present Haitian goat. The owner was proud of a converted cornhusker that served as a steering device.

"He seemed not to quite understand my reluctance to participate in this luxury Caribbean cruise, but when he hoisted sail to depart, I knew I had made the right decision. His sails were patchwork masterpieces, not a line anywhere that was not spliced every few feet. I often wonder if he ever got to Panama, or for that matter back to Port-au-Prince. I have a strong feeling that the goat had a one-way ticket."

Jack has also done his share of portrait painting, though he does not consider himself a portrait painter. "I like to do char-

"Haitian Woman"   *16″ × 20″ crayon*

Wine festival   *pen drawing*

acters and I like to do men," he says. "Women are difficult to paint. There's always something wrong with the mouth, or this or that, and because they're always changing clothes and hair styles they don't even look like the same person six months later.

"I had a lady call me once after I had delivered her picture, and she thanked me because I didn't make her nose look like a banana. She wasn't concerned that she did have a nose that looked like a banana. She wanted it to look like somebody else's nose, a nose that didn't look like a banana."

Nowadays, Jack says, the painter is competing with the camera and is expected to get a good likeness, whereas nobody is concerned whether or not the "Mona Lisa" looks like the woman who posed for it. "We don't have the slightest idea. Leonardo da Vinci fooled around with it for over four years, trying to paint the thing. He never could get rid of it. He finally sold it, and eventually it wound up in the Louvre. Here's somebody holding an enigmatic smile for four years; can you imagine a model trying to do that?

"Rembrandt's best-known painting, 'The Night Watch,' was commissioned by the Amsterdam civic guard and was supposed to have literal portraits of the whole company. However, only a few guardsmen's faces were recognizable and they were dissatisfied with the picture. Later it was cut down for the central figure. Rembrandt was paid for the painting, but his commissions fell off sharply after that.

"Everybody and his brother painted George Washington, and about the only thing we know that's accepted as coming close to looking like Washington is Houdon's statue, which was done from a mask. Peale did a number of portraits; they don't look like Gilbert Stuart's. Gilbert Stuart thought he got a pretty good likeness, and he never delivered the picture. He painted over a hundred copies from the one he did to begin with. He would copy it and sell another one, sell another one. Mrs. Washington kept writing Stuart, and he was always saying, 'Well, I haven't finished it.' It would have taken him about ten minutes to finish the bottom of the picture.

When he was commissioned to do a portrait of Admiral Richard E. Byrd, Mrs. Byrd called Jack on the telephone. "They were living in Boston, and she said she wanted to make sure that I got his 'bedroom eyes' in the picture. Well, this was fascinating to me," Jack says. "Here's a man who's internationally known as an explorer and she's worried about his 'bedroom eyes' in the portrait." And did he get the eyes right? Well, Admiral Byrd liked the picture when it was unveiled.

"That's a terrible test, to have the subject stand beside the picture when it is unveiled. I had done several portraits of Admiral Byrd, but the most recent one was commissioned by Mr. Thomas Byrd. The painting was to hang in the wardroom of the missile cruiser U.S.S. *Virginia*. Iris and I were guests of the Navy at the commissioning of the ship. After the ceremony we attended a reception for the Secretary of the Navy, Senator Byrd, and other distinguished guests.

"We were talking to Senator Byrd about the painting of the Admiral, which was displayed on a nearby easel. Suddenly two grim-faced men in dark suits stood beside me.

"'Your name Woodson?' from the first grim face.

"'Why—yes,' from a startled me.

"'Come with us, we've been looking for you.' I was marched off to a group standing across the room.

"'Mr. Woodson, meet the Secretary of the Navy, Mr. Middendorf,' said my escort.

"'Oh, yes, of course, you're the artist,' said the Secretary as we shook hands. 'Say, I certainly do like your portrait of the Admiral. How about doing one of me?'

"'Well, I . . . well, ah, why certainly,' I finally managed to get out, 'but how will there ever be time to work with you?'

"'Oh, that's easy. I'm in the Pentagon most of the time—just come on up. Here, take my tie clasp so that you won't forget me.' He removed his tie clasp and handed it to me. It was gold and carried the flag of the Secretary of the Navy.

"Fate intervened, in the form of a new administration and with it a new secretary. I never heard any more about the portrait. I still wear the Secretary's tie clasp. I'm sure he has another one."

Admiral Richard E. Byrd with Woodson portrait

Firing of cannon designed by Woodson

According to Iris, "Jack's mother once told me that if there was anything she didn't like about Jack's father, it was his sense of humor. I didn't understand, because that's supposed to be a good trait, but I've been married to Jack long enough to know what she meant, because he's exactly like his Daddy. He can see something funny in absolutely everything."

Jack seems particularly tickled at the anomalies of his own situation. "It's hard to believe what you get into, trying to please everybody, all these different people. Us Baptists, for instance. I used to do a lot of religious stuff, and we used to have to do two versions of a picture—one for the Catholics and one for the Protestants, particularly the Baptists. The Baptists wouldn't buy anything if it had a cross on the church, and the Catholics wouldn't buy it if it didn't. Presbyterians liked purple. I once had a painting of Christ returned to me with the comment, 'We know that you're probably right and the picture's just fine, but couldn't you make him look a little less Jewish?'

"You have to have a sense of humor, because it *is* funny, and so much of it is so trivial."

There are artists who are known for painting the American flag, and children with sad eyes, and pieces of pastry, and squares, and stripes, and all manner of profitable, trademarked visions of the world. This luxury is denied to painters like Jack Woodson, who have had to learn to paint almost any conceivable object or subject skillfully, in any of the convenient media.

On one occasion in Williamsburg he met Norman Rockwell, whom he'd admired ever since he had a *Saturday Evening Post* route as a small boy, keeping two cents out of every nickel he received. The two got to talking, and Jack remembers saying something like this: "Me, I've got to paint something that looks like Winslow Homer for the moment, then I do some animated stuff and it's got to look like Walt Disney; here's my Maxfield Parrish; the next one is a pen-and-ink drawing that looks like Franklin Booth. All *you* have to be is Norman Rockwell."

Even when he is painting a ship, he is haunted by everybody else who has ever painted the same subject. "I try to make the ship look like Montague Dawson painted it, but not the water. Montague Dawson was not the greatest on water. Carl Evers, he's the water painter, but his ships are tight. So I'd like to paint ships like Montague Dawson, I'd like to paint the water like Carl Evers, and I'd like to paint the sky like Gordon Grant, or like the greatest of all the Dutch marine painters, Van de Velde. You don't wind up being anybody when you try to please everybody— which you can't do, but you try."

But designing restaurants or stained-glass plates is just one line of work, albeit an enjoyable one, for Jack Woodson, whose business is primarily putting paint on canvas. He is anything but impressionistic in his methods, and there is nothing slapdash to his technique. For instance, Jack says, when painting a ship "you have to try to please the mariner, who couldn't care less about the esthetics of the sky, and try to please the arty critic, who wouldn't know a stanchion from a king post." With

Woodson and Norman Rockwell

his meticulous research and a back-up model, he is fairly sure to get the details right on the ship. For the rest, he trusts to the skill of a lifetime's experience. "There are probably more ships painted than any other subject, and there are probably more inaccurately drawn ships, too," he says. "It is amazing how many otherwise fine painters fall apart when painting a ship."

It has been both the choice and the fate of Jack Woodson to be the Local Artist all his life. "The kiss of death is being the Local Artist," he says. "They do a newspaper article about you and it starts off, 'Local Artist So-and-So'—that's the first thing. As soon as anybody reads that he thinks, 'Well, he can't be very good or what's he doing here?' I always felt if I'd come from somewhere else—like Fargo, North Dakota—it would have been better. . . ."

In fact, he has had opportunities to go other places, including an invitation to work with Disney Studios, but he and Iris have preferred to remain in Richmond. And why not? "Right now, I'm doing work for the United States Historical Society and for Royal Copenhagen/Bing & Grondahl. I've done commercial films that were shown in China, I've done documentary motion pictures that won national awards, and there's been a lot of satisfaction in all of it. I found that you really don't have to go anywhere else. They'll find you."

"I try to work just like everybody else," Jack says. "I think one of the proudest moments of my life was when I went off on a business trip with Bob Kline and I had on a three-piece suit, I had an attaché case with nothing in it, and for a brief moment, I looked like everybody else getting on and off the airplane. I looked like a perfectly normal person. When Bob opened his briefcase, I noticed he had a bunch of grapes in there. Then I even *felt* normal!

"My daughter was almost grown before she realized I was gainfully employed. Here I am out in the back yard with a youngster straddling the fence, and he's Buffalo Bill, or here I am in the middle of July setting up a Christmas tree that I'm going to work from.

"I didn't come and go, like everybody else did. I paid my own Social Security. When I go into the schools today, the young-

sters want to know about security. If you're thinking about security, I say you should get a job selling shoes, and then you can go home at five o'clock and forget it.

"I'm never off. I'm working all the time. I'll be walking along and I'll stop suddenly and somebody wants to know what I'm looking at. And I'll say, 'See that house over there, that side, see how yellow it is? I'll use that in a picture someday.' It's to my advantage to be constantly looking at how the light is hitting that house or that puddle of water. . . ."

Of the hundreds, maybe thousands, of pictures Jack has painted, does he have a favorite?

"No, the truth is you never do a favorite picture," he says.

American Indian *crayon*

"Every time you start something, it's going to be the greatest since the Sistine Chapel, and by the time you get halfway through, you're so sick of it, it's the worst. You wonder, why did I ever start this thing? And when you finally finish it, you're almost ashamed to deliver it.

"But then the next one's going to be the greatest, and of course the same thing happens. Any time you think you've painted the greatest picture, that's the end of you. The only thing you do is just keep trying to do it a little bit better each time."

"But just once," he confesses, "it would be wonderful to paint a picture just for me, and if nobody liked it, well, what difference would it make? People would say, 'I don't like it,' and I'd tell them, 'I don't care.' They'd say, 'I don't want it,' and I'd say, 'I don't want you to have it.'"

Yet this man who paints pictures so that he can sell them, who acts like a businessman and goes to the office to work, and who insists that "I'm not trying to paint the great American masterpiece," thinks the greatest painter who ever lived was Vermeer. "If reincarnation really exists," he says, "I'd like to return as Jan Vermeer of Delft.

"You know, he never sold many of his pictures. He ran an art shop, a store that sold paintings and antiques, but he never made much at painting. He died leaving 26 pictures undisposed of, and there are only 37 known Vermeers in public and private collections today. He lost several because he had to give them to the grocer to pay his bills, so in a way he was painting to eat, just like everybody else."